Water

I love water!

Sarah Ridley

W
FRANKLIN WATTS
LONDON • SYDNEY

espresso
education

First published in 2011 by
Franklin Watts
338 Euston Road
London NW1 3BH

Franklin Watts Australia
Level 17/207 Kent Street
Sydney NSW 2000

The Espresso characters are originated and designed by Claire Underwood and Pesky Ltd.

The Espresso characters are the property of Espresso Education Ltd.

A CIP catalogue record for this book is available from the British Library.

ISBN: 978 1 4451 0394 5
Dewey: 553.7

Series Editor: Sarah Peutrill
Art Director: Jonathan Hair
Series Designer: Matthew Lilly
Illustrations by Artful Doodlers Ltd.

Printed in China

Franklin Watts is a division of
Hachette Children's Books,
an Hachette UK company
www.hachette.co.uk

Picture credits: Antikainen/istockphoto: 21t. Asianet-Pakistan/Shutterstock: 16t. Luke Daniek/istockphoto: 13b. Djinn/Shutterstock: 29b. duckrabbit.info/Alamy: 14. Elena Elisseeva/Shutterstock: 19. German/istockphoto: 20. Richard Gillard/istockphoto: 27. Fred Hendricks/Shutterstock: 6b. Ann Taylor-Hughes/istockphoto: 18b. Intraclique LLC/Shutterstock: 10b. Lin Chun-Tso/istockphoto: 22b. Olga Lyubkina/Shutterstock: 28bl. Steve Maehl/Shutterstock: 23br. Musée Marmottan, Paris/Peter Willi /Superstock: 17. NASA: 5c. Pelamiswave.com: 26. Dmitry Pichugin/Shutterstock: 5t. Paul Prescott/Shutterstock: 25t. Jeremy Richards/istockphoto: 11t. Antonio S/Shutterstock: 12. Harish Tyagi/epa/Corbis: 25c. Alan Williams/NHPA: 13t.Every attempt has been made to clear copyright. Should there be any inadvertent omission please apply to the publisher for rectification.

Contents

The Espresso friends:

I'm Sal and I'm 10.

I'm Ash and I'm 8.

I'm Scully and I'm Ash's dog.

I'm Kim and I'm 7.

I'm Polly and I'm 6.

I'm Polly's brother, Eddy, and I'm 3.

I'm Scrap and I live with Polly and Eddy.

Pages with this symbol have a downloadable photocopiable sheet (see page 30).

Water!

Ash, Scully, Kim, Polly, Eddy and Scrap have been running about. They are really thirsty. Thank goodness there is drinking water in the park.

People can only survive for a few days without water.

DOG

Water is essential for life. Everything needs water to live – people, other animals and plants. That is why few animals or plants can survive in the desert.

These elephants are drinking from a waterhole in Africa.

Kim has been looking at photos of the Earth from space. Our planet, Earth, looks blue because three-quarters of its surface is covered by water. Most of the water on Earth is in the seas and oceans. It is salty and undrinkable. The rest is in icebergs, glaciers, rivers, streams, lakes, ponds, reservoirs or in groundwater.

Fast facts

- Ninety-seven per cent of all Earth's water is in the seas and oceans.
- Only three per cent of all the water on Earth is drinkable.
- Two per cent of that fresh water is locked up as ice.
- One per cent is available as fresh water.
- No other planet we know about has as much water on its surface.

Quiz:
What is a glacier?

A) A frozen mountain top

B) A frozen lake

C) A slow-moving river of ice

Quiz answers are on page 32.

Solid, liquid, gas

Sal, Kim and Polly decided to find out more about water as a material. Water is unusual as it is the only natural material on Earth that can be found as a liquid, a solid and a gas.

Water as a liquid
Liquid water pours from taps, fills our swimming pools, rains from the sky, and moves about in our oceans, rivers and reservoirs.

Water as a solid
When water cools down to freezing point, it forms solid ice. Ice cubes cool down a glass of water. Icebergs are huge pieces of frozen water.

Icebergs are huge pieces of frozen water. They form in the coldest parts of the world.

Water as a gas

When water heats up, it changes into water vapour, a gas. This process is called evaporation. Water vapour is usually invisible. The air you breathe out contains water vapour and on cold days you can see this water vapour in your breath. This is because the cold air makes the water vapour change into tiny droplets of water that look like a white cloud.

Fast facts

- Water freezes at 0°C (zero degrees Celsius).
- Ice melts at 0°C.
- Water evaporates at any temperature above freezing.
- Water boils at 100°C.

Science spot: water evaporates

Kim did an experiment. He placed three small bowls in different places – one on a sunny windowsill (or over a radiator in winter), one in the fridge and one in a dark corner. He placed an ice cube in each bowl. What do you think happened over the next week? Try his experiment and see if you were right.

The water cycle

Ash wanted to know where all the water comes from. He discovered that the same water keeps going round and round in what is called the water cycle. In fact people today are drinking the same water that was around at the time of the dinosaurs.

Ash decides to explain the water cycle to Kim by drawing a diagram.

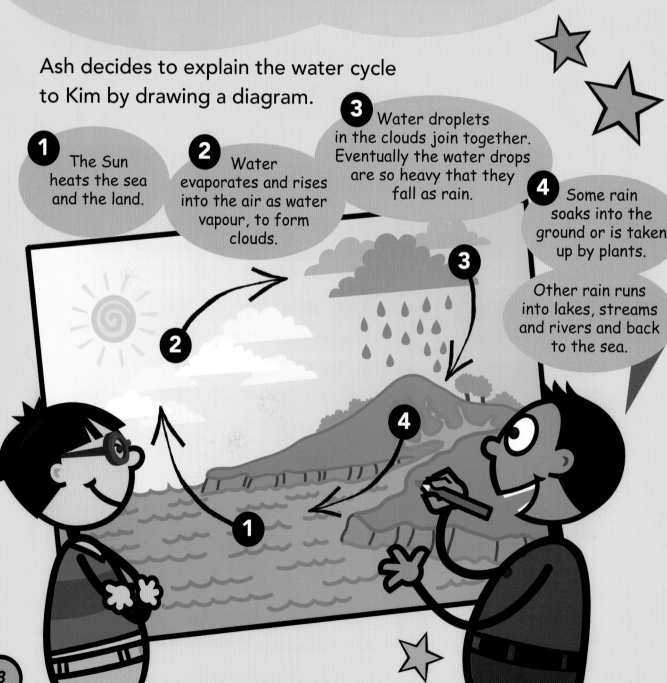

1 The Sun heats the sea and the land.

2 Water evaporates and rises into the air as water vapour, to form clouds.

3 Water droplets in the clouds join together. Eventually the water drops are so heavy that they fall as rain.

4 Some rain soaks into the ground or is taken up by plants.

Other rain runs into lakes, streams and rivers and back to the sea.

Kim showed Eddy how to make a cloud in a jam jar.

You will need:
- A large glass jar
- Warm water
- A foil pie case
- Some ice cubes
- A torch

1 Pour warm water into the jar until it is a third full.

2 Place the pie case on the opening of the jar.

3 Empty the ice cubes into the pie case.

4 Turn off any lights and shine the torch into the jar.

5 You should see your very own cloud forming!

6 Wait a few minutes and look under the pie case to see drops of water. These will fall back into the jar as 'rain'.

Snow, hail and rain

The friends like to play together. Sometimes the weather keeps them indoors and other times it makes playtime more fun.

You can't hit me!

In the winter, the friends enjoy snow. Snowflakes form inside clouds when tiny ice crystals stick to each other. They often melt as they fall but if it is cold enough they will fall as snow.

Hail stones

Last summer the friends watched an amazing thunderstorm. As the sky went dark, hail stones bounced onto the ground. These began as drops of water that were blown high into the thunderclouds where the air was freezing cold. The water froze and fell to the ground as hail stones.

Hail stones can be small or large. The heaviest one ever found weighed over a kilogramme!

Geography spot: monsoon rains

Kim's family went to India this summer to visit friends. The monsoon had just finished. The monsoon occurs when strong winds bring heavy rainfall to the country. It rains for days, reservoirs fill up  and the countryside turns green. Find out more about the monsoon season, the hurricane season or the cyclone season that occur in different countries around the world.

Quiz:
What is precipitation?

A) The edge of a cliff

B) When liquid water turns into water vapour

C) The name for falling rain, hail, sleet and snow

Feedback...
What is your favourite weather? Why?

Rivers

Ash and Scully enjoy walks beside the river, whatever the weather. Sometimes they get wet! When rain falls from the clouds, some of it runs across the ground into streams and rivers.

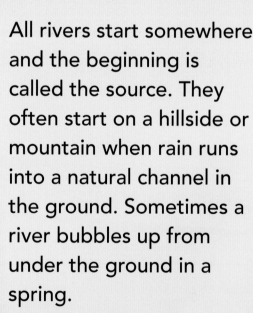

All rivers start somewhere and the beginning is called the source. They often start on a hillside or mountain when rain runs into a natural channel in the ground. Sometimes a river bubbles up from under the ground in a spring.

A mountain stream works its way around rocks and boulders.

A river always runs downhill to the sea. Along its way, the river winds across the landscape, usually getting wider. At the coast, the river forms an estuary and this is where river water and seawater join. River estuaries attract masses of birds, especially at low tide.

At low tide wading birds feed on worms, shellfish and tiny animals that live in the estuary mud.

History spot: the River Nile

The ancient Egyptians lived along the banks of the River Nile. Once a year the river flooded, leaving thick, black mud good for growing crops. The people also used the Nile for transport and trade, and to catch fish. They even built their boats from tall reeds that grew beside the river.

Feedback...

Do you like walking by water? How can you keep safe by water?

Egyptian farmers continue to grow crops on the banks of the River Nile although modern dams prevent the Nile from flooding as it once did.

Floods

Sal's classmates have been writing letters to schoolchildren in Bangladesh. Once a year it rains for days during the monsoon until rivers flood the land. Floods are part of life there.

Sal received this letter from Bangladesh:

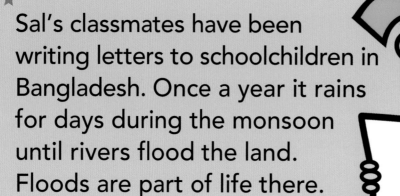

This is me, Abdul

Abdul
The house on stilts
Bangladesh

25th September

Dear Sal
Thank you for your letter.
My home is built on stilts to protect us from flood water. Recently a flood shelter was built in my village on the highest bit of ground. It is even higher off the ground than my home and gives us safety if the flood waters are very high. If there is a storm coming, a neighbour hears about it on his radio and warns us all.

Write back and tell me more about you!
Abdul

These people have saved what they can from rising flood waters in Pakistan.

Floods can be very dangerous in Bangladesh and all round the world. Some people drown or are killed by moving objects in the fast-flowing water. The flood waters destroy homes, roads and crops, leaving people without shelter, clean drinking water or food.

Maths spot: Bangladesh bar chart

I've started this bar chart of the rainfall in Dhaka.

Make a bar chart to show the usual rainfall in Dhaka, the capital of Bangladesh, over a year. Write the months along the bottom and the rainfall measurements in millimetres up the side: Jan: 18, Feb: 31, March: 58, April: 103, May: 194, June: 321, July: 437, Aug: 305, Sept: 254, Oct: 169, Nov: 28, Dec: 2.

Add up the rainfall during the monsoon months (June to September).

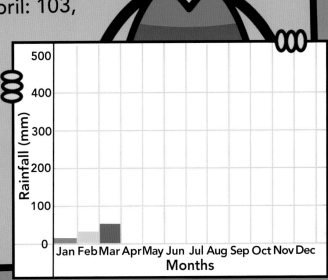

Painting water

Sal often paints pictures at home. She has been looking at some paintings of water by the French painter, Claude Monet. He painted many seascapes and river scenes as well as his famous water gardens filled with water lilies.

1 Have a look at some paintings by Impressionist artists, including Claude Monet. Look in detail at how the water has been painted. Which colours has the artist used?

You will need:

- Watercolours or paintbox
- Pencil and rubber
- Sheets of paper
- Paintbrushes
- Jar of water

2 Choose some paper for a river painting or seascape.

3 Sketch out the scene. Ask an adult to take you on a trip to a river or beach, or use photographs to give you ideas.

4 What materials will you use to add colour? Watercolours work well. Try them out on a separate piece of paper before you set to work on your painting.

5 With watercolours you could try this wet-on-wet style of painting. Paint the paper with clean water first. Then when you add paint the colours will blend together.

Fast facts: Impressionists

- Impressionist artists were at work about 150 years ago, mostly in France.
- They often began their paintings outside, rather than in a studio.
- They worked quickly to paint the colour and light they saw before them.
- They included Claude Monet, Auguste Renoir, Camille Pissarro and Edgar Degas.

Monet's painting *Impression, Sunrise* helped to give the Impressionist painters their name.

Drinking water

Kim turned on the tap, filled a glass with water and wondered how it got there. He decided to investigate and wrote a report for school.

I wonder how this water reached my tap.

From rain cloud to tap

When it rains some of the water runs into rivers and streams, or into underground water stores. In turn, some of the rivers and streams fill up reservoirs, which are huge storage places for water. The water company pipes water from a reservoir, or from an underground water store, into the water works.

At the water works, the water needs to be cleaned up. So the water is filtered, cleaned, checked, tested and then allowed to pass into huge water pipes. Under the ground, the water travels in pipes to schools, shops and businesses and into our homes!

Vast reservoirs store water to supply the homes in the local cities, towns and villages.

Geography spot: settlements and water

People need a good source of drinking water. In the past, many villages, towns and cities grew up beside rivers or springs. If a place outgrew its water supply, water was piped or channelled in. What else makes people settle in one place rather than another?

The ancient Romans built this aqueduct in Nîmes, France to bring a supply of drinking water to the town.

Quiz:
How many drinks should you drink every day?

The same amount as about:

A) Six glasses of water

B) Twelve glasses of water

C) One glass of water

Down the drain

Kim and Ash listen to the water rushing down the pipes after they have washed their hands for lunch. They learnt what happens to waste water on a recent school trip to the local waste water treatment works.

The dirty water is cleaned up in several stages at the waste water treatment works.

First they saw the waste water arrive at the site. It had travelled along underground pipes from homes, schools and other buildings. Screens filtered out pieces of paper, cloth, litter or twigs. Then the dirty water flowed on to the next stage.

It smells a bit pongy round here!

Fast facts

- The first waste water treatment works in the UK was built 160 years ago.
- Bacteria do most of the cleaning up work at a waste water treatment works.
- Some power stations burn sludge to produce electricity.

They saw several tanks. In some of them, solids were sinking to the bottom to form sludge. The sludge is then treated in a separate area where bacteria break it down to make it safe. In other tanks, the dirty water was being filtered and treated.

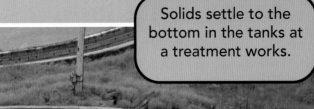

Solids settle to the bottom in the tanks at a treatment works.

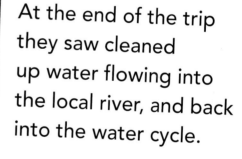

This place is huge!

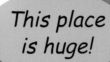

At the end of the trip they saw cleaned up water flowing into the local river, and back into the water cycle.

PSHE spot: water for all

Billions of people around the world do not have homes with working toilets or drinking water piped to their homes. Perhaps you could organise an event to raise money for WaterAid, an organisation that works to change this situation.

Water and plants

Kim, Ash and Polly have been watering the school garden. They know that without water the plants will wilt and die.

Most plants survive in the wild as long as it rains regularly. When farmers grow crops, they need to make sure the plants grow at their best. So if it doesn't rain enough, they irrigate – they bring water to the fields in channels or pipes, or pump it out of a nearby river.

With irrigation, farmers can grow crops through hot weather or in places where little rain falls.

Polly likes growing seeds. She prepared three saucers with a layer of paper tissue. She sprinkled a few cress seeds onto each one and put them all on a window-sill.

1 2 3

She didn't water the first one at all, the second she watered just once at the beginning and the third she watered regularly. Look at the pictures to see how they grew.

Cool!

Cacti can store water, in order to survive long periods of time without rain.

? Feedback...

Do you like planting seeds and caring for plants?
What have you grown?

Sacred water

Polly and Eddy went to a baptism at the weekend. They watched the vicar scoop some water onto the baby's head. That made the baby cry!

In the Christian baptism service, water is used to wash away sin. Then the person can be welcomed into the Christian Church. The Christian holy book, the Bible, tells the story of how Jesus was baptised in the River Jordan. He went right under the water, which still happens in some Christian baptism services today.

Muslims pray five times a day and they must make sure they are clean before they begin prayers. Mosques have washrooms where people can clean their faces, mouths, feet and arms, using plenty of clean water.

The Muslims' special way of washing before prayers is called 'wudu'.

Every 12 years, millions of people travel to the River Ganges to wash away their sins at the great Kumbh Mela, the world's biggest religious festival.

In the Hindu religion there are several sacred rivers, including the River Ganges in India. Hindus believe that if they bathe in the River Ganges or another sacred river they will wash away their sins.

Without water there would be no life on Earth, which is one of the reasons why water is important in religions worldwide. Water also washes away dirt. How is water being used in the photos on this page?

Powerful water

Ash visited an old water mill at the weekend. He watched the water turn the water wheel round and round. The water wheel made machinery grind flour inside the mill.

History spot: water mills

In Tudor times, water mills were often used to grind wheat into flour. The local landowner usually owned the mill. When a family brought their grain harvest to the mill, they had to give some of the flour to the mill owner as payment. Flour was made into bread, which the Tudors ate with every meal.

I love the wooshing noise.

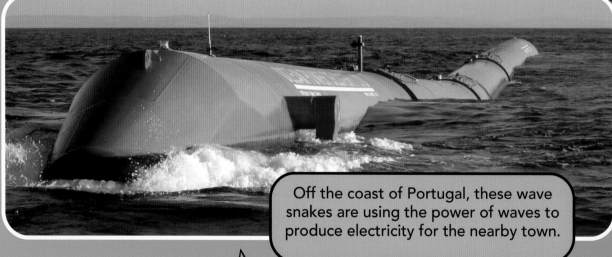

Off the coast of Portugal, these wave snakes are using the power of waves to produce electricity for the nearby town.

Ash decided to research and write an article for the school newspaper about water power today.

Espresso Extra

Our reporter, Ash, investigates water power.

HYDRO-ELECTRIC POWER

Hydro-electric power is electricity generated by moving water. The water spins turbines that power a generator to produce electricity. The great news is that hydro-electric power stations do not release polluting gases into the air and water will never run out.

There are three main ways of producing electricity from water. Usually, a power company builds a huge dam with a reservoir behind it. As water is released through the dam, it turns the turbines. In some places, long barrages are built across wide rivers or river estuaries. As the tides rise and fall, water turns turbines in the barrage. Finally there are various types of wave machine that turn the movement of the waves into power.

The bad news is that dams and barrages are expensive to build and can harm wildlife. Wave power could be a good way of producing electricity in the future but it costs a lot to set up. Some countries, like Norway, already get almost all their power from hydro-electric power stations.

Water for fun

Ash loves to swim in the sea while Eddy likes paddling. Scrap and Scully get very excited by the waves!

There are many ways that people have fun on water. Recently, Sal enjoyed an afternoon out with her parents in a canoe. They all wore life jackets in case they fell in the river. She would like to learn to snorkel or sail one day.

There are several different water sports. Have you ever tried rowing, surfing, sailing, diving, water-skiing or kayaking? It is also fun to go on nature trips to watery habitats. One day perhaps you can go out in a boat to see whales, seals, dolphins or other animals that live in water.

Swimming is a sport which uses most of the body so it is a good form of exercise. It builds up muscle strength, makes the heart and lungs work hard and improves stamina.

If you take lessons, you will improve your strokes. This will allow you to enjoy visits to the sea or to the pool much more, and it will keep you safe should you ever fall into deep water. You could join a swimming club and enter swimming competitions. You never know – you might even make it to the Olympics one day.

Swimming in the sea is fun but always make sure that an adult is watching you.

Glossary

ancient Egyptians The people who lived along the banks of the River Nile in Egypt from around 5,000 years ago.

bacteria Tiny living things that are all around us.

barrage A barrier built across a river to control the flow of water.

church Place where Christians go to worship.

dam A barrier built to keep back water.

estuary The wide part of a river where it flows into the sea.

evaporation The process where a liquid, such as water, changes into a vapour or gas.

filter To pour a liquid through a material to separate out any small bits.

flood When water overflows onto land that is usually dry.

glacier A slow-moving river of ice.

groundwater Water held underground in springs or rocks.

Jesus The man whose life and teachings form the basis of the Christian religion.

Kumbh Mela This Hindu festival takes place on the River Ganges in India every three years. Every twelve years, the huge great Kumbh Mela occurs.

mosque The place where Muslims go to worship.

natural material Any product or material that comes from the land, sea or ground. This includes oil, water, wood and metals.

Olympics The international sports competition held every four years.

precipitation Any form of water falling from the sky as rain, snow, sleet or hail.

reservoir A large area used to store water.

sacred An object or a place seen to be very special, or holy.

sewage Human waste.

sin A bad action, word or thought against the laws of a religion.

source A place where a river begins.

spring A place where water pushes up from underground.

tides The movement of the water in seas and tidal rivers, caused by the invisible pull of the Moon.

turbine A machine with blades that spin around in water or air to turn a generator and produce electricity.

waterhole A natural hollow containing water.

water vapour Water in the form of a gas.

Activity sheets

Go to www.franklinwatts.co.uk/downloads for free worksheets. Pages 8–9 A template of the water cycle to label. Page 15 A sheet that helps you calculate your family's water usage in a day.

Espresso connections

Here are a few ideas for how to take the contents of this book further using Espresso.

Water! (pages 4–5)

The *Wonderful World*, video in *Geography 2 > Mountains > Natural environments* could help introduce the subject. The *Assemblies* collection in *News* includes a ready-made assembly on the theme of water. In the *News archive* in *Science 2 > The Earth and beyond > Planets*, there are several news stories about the search for water and therefore whether life could exist on Mars.

Solid, liquid, gas (pages 6–7)

Explore the three states of water further in *Science 2 > Investigating change*.

The water cycle (pages 8–9)

For a video about the water cycle, go to *ICT 2 > Computer modelling > Water supply > The water cycle*. There is also an online book on the water cycle in *English 2 > Big books*. For further resources, try the video and activities *Rain, Rain, Rain* in *Maths 2 > Measures: Challenge zone > Level 3: Data*.

Snow, hail and rain (pages 10–11)

Find out about weather in *Science 2 > Earth, Moon and Sun > Seasons* and *Geography 2 > Natural disasters*. For detailed information about the weather in countries around the world, use *Passport* in *Geography 2*. When students have found out about the weather in different places around the world, they could then write a postcard as if they have visited.

Rivers (pages 12–13)

For a detailed look at the River Usk in Wales, go to *Geography 2 > Investigating rivers*. In *History 2 >* *Egyptians*, there is a video about the Nile and its importance. The photos include a wall painting of hunting in the reeds and a tomb model of a boat.

Floods (pages 14–15)

For information about recent flood disasters, use the *Natural disasters* interactive map in *Geography 2*. In *News 2 archive > Geography > Environmental issues* there is an article about World Water Day. In *ICT 2 > Computer modelling*, the *Water At Home* interactive model looks at how to cut down water use. There is also a printable *Water at Home audit* in *Find out more*.

Painting water (pages 16–17)

For information on Impressionist artists, including Monet, use *Art and Design 2 > Artists Collection > Impressionists*. Use *Art 2 > A sense of place > Techniques > Paint and brushes* to explore different types of paint, including watercolours. The *River landscapes* in *Art 2* focuses on rivers in paintings and poems, with ideas for activities.

Drinking water (pages 18–19)

ICT 2 > Computer modelling > Water supply has several videos about how clean water reaches our taps, and one on water supply around the world. Use the article in *News 2 archive 2 > PSHE > Healthy living > More > Water in class* to explore the importance of drinking enough water during the school day.

Down the drain (pages 20–21)

Try the writing exercise in *English 2 Writers' Workshop > Pumping station > Flush It!* Visit the *News 2 archive > History > Victorian Britain* for a look at the anniversary of the Great Stink in London. In *ICT 2 > Computer modelling* there are tips on saving water in the video *Water at Home*, as well as a printable *Water at Home Audit* in *Find out more*.

Water and plants (pages 22–23)

Watch seeds grow in *Science 2 > Digital microscope > Life cycles*. For information on different habitats, both local and regional, visit *Science 2 > Habitats*. The *New life* resource box in *Science 1* includes a video showing cress seeds growing.

Sacred water (pages 24–25)

The *News 2 archive > RE* includes stories about the Kumbh Mela in India and also shows ritual washing during Ramadan in Indonesia. *RE 2* has detailed information about each of the main world religions.

Powerful water (pages 26–27)

In *Science 2 > Electricity > Making Electricity* there is an explanation of how turbines work and also a video about tidal power. The Library in *Geography 2 > Sustainability* has a news story about a tidal turbine in Northern Ireland as well as material on climate change. To find local water mills in your area, start with *Geography 2 > Maps and mapping > Learning tools > Symbols*. For ideas on writing newspaper reports, go to *English 2 > Newspapers*.

Water for fun (pages 28–29)

For detailed information about swimming, go to *PE 2 > Swimming and water safety*. There are also news stories in the *PE 2 > News archive* relating to swimming and outdoor and adventure activities.

Index

Quiz answers

Page 5: C) A slow-moving river of ice

Page 11: C) The name for falling rain, hail, sleet and snow

Page 19: A) Drink about six glasses of water, milk, fruit juice or soft drinks a day for good health. Water is the best choice for your teeth. Drink more in hot weather or after exercising.

These are the lists of contents for each title in *Espresso Ideas Box!*:

Chocolate
Where does chocolate come from? • How do cacao trees grow? • Cacao farming • The history of chocolate • Make a collage of the Aztec chocolate god • The chocolate trade • Make a chocolate piñata • Manufacturing chocolate • Is chocolate good for me? • Melting chocolate • Make chocolate leaves • Chocolate recipes • Chocolate heaven • Glossary and Activity sheets • Espresso connections

Light
Light in the sky • Day and night • The Sun and seasons • Shadow play • Understanding eclipses • Light for life • Seeds and shoots • Rainbows • Make a rainbow spinner • Painting light • Turn the light on! • How do we see? • Holy light • Glossary and Activity sheets • Espresso connections

Rainforests
What is a rainforest? • Rainforests around the world • Rainforest river • Life on the forest floor • Up in the trees • Play the music of the rainforest • Colourful rainforests • Animals in danger • Make a rainforest game • People of the rainorest • Disappearing rainforests • Save the rainforest • Have a rainforest debate • Glossary and Activity sheets • Espresso connections

The Olympics
The Olympic Games • The ancient Olympics • Events at the ancient Olympics • The modern Olympics • Design an Olympic kit • All about the events • Track and field • The Winter Olympics • The Paralympics • Games around the world • What makes an Olympic champion? • Medals and world records • Make an Olympics board game • Glossary and Activity sheets • Espresso connections • Index and quiz answers

Water
Water! • Solid, liquid, gas • The water cycle • Snow, hail and rain • Rivers • Floods • Painting water • Drinking water • Down the drain • Water and plants • Sacred water • Powerful water • Water for fun • Glossary and Activity sheets • Espresso connections

Where you live
What is special about where you live? • Finding out about the past • What is the natural history of your area? • The square metre project • What can maps tell us? • Make a map stick • Changes to your area • Who lives in your area? • What jobs do people do? • Make a picture quiz • What problems are there in your area? • Famous connections • Attracting visitors to your area • Glossary and Activity sheets • Espresso connections